THE Any One Can COOKBOOK

THE *Any One Can* COOKBOOK

HAMLYN

First published in 1995 by Hamlyn
an imprint of Reed Consumer Books Limited
Michelin House, 81 Fulham Road, London, SW3 6RB
and Auckland, Melbourne, Singapore and Toronto.

ISBN 0 600 58883 1

A CIP catalogue record for this book is available at the British Library.
Printed in Hong Kong.

ACKNOWLEDGEMENTS

Art Manager Bryan Dunn
Design The Design Revolution
Executive Editor Susan Haynes
Editors Maggie Ramsay, Imogen Ellis
Production Controller Melanie Frantz
Home Economist Alison Caygill
Stylist Sue Russell
Photographs Nick Carman
Sticky Toffee Pudding and Banoffi Pie Laurie Evans
Raspberry and Amaretto Fools, Coconut Ice Cream and Crème Caramel Ken Field

Recipes created by Nestlé Home Economics Department
For further information about Nestlé products please write to:
Nestlé Consumer Services, PO Box 207, York YO1 1XY.

NOTES

Both metric and imperial measurements have been given in all recipes. Use one set of measurements only and not a mixture of both, as they are not interchangeable.

Standard level spoon measurements are used in all recipes.
1 tablespoon = one 15ml spoon
1 teaspoon = one 5ml spoon

Ovens should be preheated to the specific temperature – if using a fan assisted oven, follow the manufacturer's instructions for adjusting the time and temperature.

Eggs should be size 3 unless otherwise stated.

Fresh herbs should be used unless otherwise stated. If unavailable use dried herbs as an alternative but halve the quantities stated.

CONTENTS

Any One Can

A truly convenient 'convenience food' – **Nestlé** Milks and Cream well deserve their place in every storecupboard. Of course, they can be poured over fruit and hot or cold puddings, or used for sweetmaking, or as a handy and long-lasting substitute for fresh milk and cream. But why stop there? This book demonstrates their versatility in a mouthwatering collection of more than 45 delicious sweet and savoury recipes, with beautiful photographs that will make you want to rush to the kitchen and start cooking.

Created with today's busy cook in mind, the recipes are easy to follow, quick to prepare and designed to make the most of storecupboard ingredients. There are ideas for all occasions, from warming Pumpkin and Leek Soup and Exotic Coconut Chicken Curry – ideal for an impromptu dinner party – to the Ultimate Sticky Toffee Pudding and ever-popular Gooey Chocolate Brownies. Some are variations of old favourites or classic dishes made simple; others reflect contemporary cooking at its most imaginative.

Above all, in this book **Nestlé** have collected their best-ever recipes for toffee, fudge and other sweet treats and added an invaluable section summing up all you need to know about successful sweetmaking.

Whether you view **Nestlé** Milks and Cream as convenient alternatives to fresh dairy products or appreciate them for their unique flavours and versatile cooking properties, we hope that you will soon be adding some of these wonderful recipes to your repertoire of favourite dishes.

An introduction to Nestlé Milks and Cream

Nestlé Milk was one of the very first convenience foods ever invented. Before refrigeration and today's rapid transport, fresh milk was not readily available commercially, but the goodness of milk has long been recognised, providing an important source of protein, carbohydrate, fat and calcium. In fact, it was Napoleon who originally thought of the idea of condensing milk, as he wanted to find a simple way to nourish his soldiers. However, it was not until 1856 that condensed milk became commercially available. **Nestlé** Milk went on to play an important role in World War I, when it was supplied to the soldiers in the trenches as a valuable source of energy. In World War II it was often the only form of milk available to soldiers fighting in Europe and the Far East, as it could be parachuted to them without damaging the product.

Today, **Nestlé** Sweetened Condensed Milk, **Nestlé** Cream, **Carnation** Evaporated Milk and **Carnation** Lite are enjoyed all over the world. Used imaginatively they can be incorporated into a variety of dishes and need no longer be viewed merely as convenient substitutes for fresh milk or cream, or as a topping for fruit and other puddings and desserts, as the wonderful collection of recipes in this book will demonstrate.

In recent years the emphasis on looking and feeling healthy has become even stronger and diet and health have become synonymous. Milk and cream are among the richest sources of calcium – essential for strong and healthy bones and teeth – as well as other important nutrients. **Nestlé** Milks and Cream are natural products and, as in fresh milk and cream, the nutritional content may vary from batch to batch. However, Vitamin D, which is needed to help the body absorb or metabolise calcium, is added to all the **Nestlé** Milks and Cream products, so the amount remains constant.

Nestlé Sweetened Condensed Milk

Nestlé Sweetened Condensed Milk is pure full cream cow's milk which has been pasteurised and preserved only by concentration and the addition of sugar. The special blend of milk and sugar gives **Nestlé** Milk its unique taste, perfect for making a wide variety of homemade sweets and desserts. It can be used straight out of the can and some sweet recipes do not even require cooking, so they are easy to prepare.

It is available in two can sizes: 397g and 218g.

Carnation Evaporated Milk

Carnation Evaporated Milk contains the concentrated goodness of cow's milk, with added Vitamin D. To make one 410g can of **Carnation** takes nearly two pints of fresh milk, and it can be diluted, 1.5 parts water to 1 part **Carnation**, for use in any recipe requiring fresh milk. In recipes calling for cream it can be used undiluted.

Carnation Evaporated Milk has a high solids content, which means that it is excellent for thickening, lends a wonderful creamy richness to savoury sauces and can be whipped up to three times its original volume. Whipping is particularly easy if the can is chilled in the refrigerator for at least four hours. Please note, however, that because **Carnation** Milk is a natural product, it does vary from can to can and you may find that some cans whip more easily than others.

Carnation can be used to make delicious homemade yogurt (see page 74), which is cheaper, thicker and creamier than the shop-bought variety. It also makes a beautiful shiny glaze if brushed over bread, scones, pastry or biscuits before you pop them in the oven.
It is available in two can sizes: 410g and 170g.

Carnation Lite

In response to the ever-increasing interest in healthy eating and slimming, **Nestlé** have introduced **Carnation** Lite, a delicious evaporated semi-skimmed milk which has no added sugar, preservatives or colouring and contains less than half the fat and 25% fewer calories than traditional **Carnation** Evaporated Milk. Where suitable **Carnation** Lite has been suggested for many of the sweet and savoury dishes in this book.
It is available in two sizes: 410g can and 200ml carton.

Nestlé Cream

Nestlé Cream is a convenient and long-lasting alternative to fresh cream – it can be stored for up to two years – and is a very versatile ingredient. If you need single cream, just thin down **Nestlé** Cream with a little fresh milk. For piping as a dessert topping, or as a filling for cakes or éclairs, refrigerate an unopened can of **Nestlé** Cream for two or three hours. Then, without shaking it, open the can and drain off any liquid (whey), and pipe the remaining thick cream. **Nestlé** Cream can also be used in soups, sauces and other hot dishes without any risk of curdling. Containing only 23% fat, compared with a minimum of 35% fat in fresh whipping cream and 48% fat in double cream, **Nestlé** Cream offers an ideal alternative for the health-conscious cook.
It is available in two can sizes: 170g and 283g.

Soups and Suppers

Bacon and Vegetable Frittata

Any number of variations are possible with this quick supper dish: add sliced red peppers, diced boiled potatoes, drained canned artichoke hearts or blanched sliced leeks. Frittata is delicious served with a crisp green salad.

Serves 4
Preparation time: 10 minutes
Cooking time: 10 minutes

1 tablespoon oil

1 red onion, thickly sliced

100g (4oz) streaky bacon, chopped

2 courgettes, thickly sliced

150g (6oz) mushrooms, halved

2 eggs, beaten

170g can **Carnation** Evaporated Milk or 200ml carton **Carnation** Lite

1 tablespoon pesto, optional

salt and black pepper

1 Heat the oil in a wide, heavy-bottomed frying pan and fry the onion, bacon, courgettes and mushrooms until cooked through.

2 Preheat the grill.

3 Beat together the remaining ingredients, add seasoning and pour into the frying pan, reduce the heat and cook until the egg mixture begins to set.

4 Finish off by placing the pan under a hot grill for 3-4 minutes until browned. Cool slightly, carefully remove the frittata from the pan, cut into wedges and serve hot.

Cheese Twisters

Perfect party food for all ages, these light biscuits with a hidden tang are also great as pre-dinner nibbles or as an accompaniment to soup.

Makes 24
Preparation time: 15 minutes
Cooking time: 12 minutes

225g (8oz) plain flour

1 teaspoon mustard powder

100g (4oz) butter, chilled and cut into cubes

100g (4oz) mature Cheddar cheese, grated

170g can **Carnation** Evaporated Milk

1 tablespoon yeast extract

1 Preheat the oven to 190°C (375°F), Gas Mark 5. Grease 2 baking sheets.

2 Sift the flour and mustard powder together into a large bowl, rub in the butter and stir in the grated cheese. Reserve 2 tablespoons of the **Carnation** Milk and stir the remainder into the flour mixture. Mix lightly to form a soft dough.

3 On a lightly floured surface, roll the dough into a large rectangle about 5mm (¼ inch) thick. Spread the yeast extract over half the rectangle, then fold half the dough over so that the yeast extract is inside. Roll the dough out again into a long rectangle and cut into 24 strips.

4 Twist each strip before placing on the prepared baking sheets and brush with the remaining **Carnation** Milk. Bake for 10-12 minutes, until golden. Leave to cool on a wire rack.

NOTE: If wished, shape 4 strips of pastry into individual circles and bake until golden. Once cool use the collars to hold bundles of straws together.

Leek and Pumpkin Soup

Here is a simple recipe to take advantage of the glowing orange pumpkins you can find in the market or supermarket.

Serves 4-6
Preparation time: 10 minutes
Cooking time: 40 minutes

1 large leek, trimmed, washed and sliced

900g (2lb) fresh pumpkin, peeled, deseeded and diced or 2 x 400g/450g canned pumpkin

900ml (1½ pints) chicken stock

410g can **Carnation** Evaporated Milk

½ teaspoon celery salt

salt and pepper

croûtons, to serve

1 Place the leek, fresh pumpkin and stock in a large saucepan. Bring to the boil and simmer for 30 minutes. Alternatively, if fresh pumpkin is not available, in a pan simmer the leek and stock for 15 minutes before adding the canned pumpkin.

2 Leave to cool for 5-10 minutes, then place in a liquidizer or a food processor and blend until smooth. Return to the pan and stir in the remaining ingredients.

3 Heat through over a low heat, stirring frequently. Taste and adjust the seasoning if necessary. Serve with croûtons.

NOTE:

Homemade Croûtons
Remove the crusts from 4 thick slices of day-old bread. Cut all of the bread into cubes. Heat 4 tablespoons of olive oil in a frying pan. When the oil is hot add the bread. Stir-fry for 2-3 minutes until the bread cubes are golden and crisp on all sides. Remove the croûtons from the pan with a slotted spoon and drain thoroughly on paper towels, to remove any excess oil.

Spinach and Cauliflower Soup

A creamy vegetable soup that is lower in fat than a traditional recipe using cream.

Serves 4-6
Preparation time: 10 minutes
Cooking time: 25 minutes

50g (2oz) butter

150g (6oz) frozen chopped spinach, thawed

1 onion, finely chopped

150g (6oz) cauliflower florets, chopped

25g (1oz) flour

600ml (1 pint) chicken stock

410g can **Carnation** Evaporated Milk

pinch of nutmeg

black pepper

croûtons, to serve

1 Melt the butter in a large saucepan, and add the spinach, onion and cauliflower.

2 Stir in the flour, remove the pan from the heat and gradually blend in the stock.

3 Bring to the boil, stirring frequently, until the mixture thickens. Stir in the **Carnation** Milk, nutmeg and seasoning. Cover and simmer for 15-20 minutes.

4 Place in a liquidizer or food processor and blend until smooth. Taste and adjust the seasoning if necessary. Serve with croûtons.

NOTE:

Homemade Croûtons
See recipe on page 14.

Chicken and Ham Pie

A satisfying pie that is best served with green vegetables and boiled, mashed or baked potatoes.

Serves 4-6
Preparation time: 20 minutes
Cooking time: 25 minutes

25g (1oz) butter

450g (1lb) chicken breast, diced

225g (8oz) cooked ham or bacon, diced

2 carrots, diced

100g (4oz) button mushrooms

300ml (½ pint) white wine

410g can **Carnation** Evaporated Milk

150ml (¼ pint) chicken stock

25g (1oz) flour

black pepper

225g (8oz) puff pastry

milk or beaten egg, to glaze

1 Preheat the oven to 200°C (400°F), Gas Mark 6.

2 Melt the butter in a large pan and brown the chicken and ham or bacon. Add the carrots and mushrooms and fry for 5 minutes. Stir in the white wine and turn up the heat so the wine boils and reduces by half.

3 Meanwhile, mix the **Carnation** Milk with the stock. Blend a little milk with the flour to form a smooth paste. Stir in the remaining **Carnation** mixture. Gradually add to the pan, stirring continuously, until the sauce boils and thickens. Season, then transfer to a 1.1 litre (2 pint) pie dish.

4 Roll out the pastry on a lightly floured surface. Use to cover the pie; moisten the edges to ensure the pastry is well sealed.

5 Brush with milk or beaten egg to glaze, then bake for 25 minutes or until the pastry is golden brown. Serve immediately.

Balti Chicken Curry

The balti pan, from northern India and Pakistan, is similar to the Chinese wok. It is used for quickly cooked curries, such as this spicy chicken dish.

Serves 4
Preparation time: 15 minutes
Cooking time: 25-30 minutes

4 tablespoons oil

2 teaspoons cardamom pods

½ teaspoon ground cloves

2 teaspoons cumin seeds

1 onion, grated

2 fresh green chillies, deseeded and very finely chopped

½ teaspoon turmeric

½ teaspoon paprika

2 tablespoons ground coriander

2 teaspoons salt

450g (1lb) boneless, skinless chicken breasts, cubed

410g can **Carnation** Evaporated Milk

fresh coriander leaves, to garnish

naan bread, to serve

1 Heat the oil in a wok or a large frying pan and add the cardamom pods, ground cloves and cumin seeds. As soon as the spices start to pop, add the onion and chillies and fry for 3-4 minutes, stirring occasionally, until the onions have softened.

2 Add the turmeric, paprika, ground coriander, salt and chicken pieces and quickly fry over a high heat, stirring constantly until the chicken pieces are golden.

3 Add the **Carnation** Milk and 250ml (8 fl oz) water and simmer, uncovered, for 15-20 minutes.

4 Serve hot, garnished with freshly chopped coriander and accompanied by warmed naan bread.

NOTE: This is a medium-hot curry, if you would prefer a milder alternative see recipe for Coconut Chicken Curry on page 30.

Tortiglioni with Tuna and Tomato

A quick pasta dish to make the most of storecupboard ingredients.

Serves 4
Preparation time: 10 minutes
Cooking time: 15 minutes

350g (12oz) tortiglioni pasta shapes

1 tablespoon oil

1 clove garlic, crushed

1 onion, chopped

400g can chopped tomatoes

2 tablespoons tomato purée or sun-dried tomato paste

50g (2oz) black olives, (optional)

200g can tuna, drained and broken into chunks

170g can **Carnation** Evaporated Milk or 200ml carton **Carnation** Lite

salt and black pepper

shavings of fresh Parmesan cheese, to serve (optional)

1 Cook the tortiglioni in a large saucepan filled with plenty of boiling salted water for 10-15 minutes, according to the packet instructions, until it is *al dente* (just tender).

2 Meanwhile, heat the oil in a saucepan over a low heat and gently fry the garlic and onion until softened, stirring constantly to ensure they do not brown. Add the remaining ingredients, except the **Carnation** Milk or Lite, season well and simmer for 10 minutes.

3 Stir in the **Carnation** Milk or Lite and return to the boil.

4 Drain the pasta well and toss in the sauce. Serve at once, sprinkled with the shavings of fresh Parmesan cheese, if liked.

Golden Fish Bake

A simple, healthy fish pie for every day meals – or add scallops for a special occasion.

Serves 4
Preparation time: 30 minutes
Cooking time: 35 minutes

675g (1½lb) potatoes, peeled

675g (1½lb) mixed fish, e.g. peeled prawns and skinned and cubed cod or haddock

410g can **Carnation** Evaporated Milk

25g (1oz) butter

25g (1oz) flour

150ml (¼ pint) white wine

4 tablespoons freshly chopped parsley

150g (6oz) Emmental or Cheddar cheese, grated

salt and black pepper

1 Preheat the oven to 200°C (400°F), Gas Mark 6.

2 Boil the potatoes in salted water until just tender. Drain, allow to cool, and then dice. Place the selection of fish in a 1.1 litre (2 pint) shallow ovenproof dish.

3 Heat the **Carnation** Milk, butter, flour and wine in a saucepan, whisking continuously until the sauce boils and thickens. Stir in the chopped parsley, 75g (3oz) of the cheese and the seasoning.

4 Pour the sauce over the fish and top with the diced potatoes and the remaining cheese. Bake for 30-35 minutes, until golden.

Danish Blue Cheese and Spinach Quiche

A vegetarian main course that holds plenty of appeal for meat-eaters.

Serves 8
Preparation time: 15 minutes
Cooking time: 40 minutes

225g (8oz) shortcrust pastry

25g (1oz) butter

1 small onion, chopped

225g (8oz) frozen chopped spinach, thawed

75g (3oz) Danish Blue cheese, crumbled

4 eggs, size 2

410g can **Carnation** Evaporated Milk

salt and freshly ground black pepper

1 Preheat the oven to 200°C (400°F), Gas Mark 6.

2 Roll out the pastry and line a 23cm (9 inch) round, deep flan tin. Chill for 20 minutes, then bake blind (see page 78) for 15 minutes.

3 Melt the butter in a saucepan, add the onion and fry until softened. Stir in the spinach and cook for a further 2 minutes. Spread the spinach mixture over the base of the pastry case. Scatter over the crumbled Danish Blue cheese.

4 In a bowl beat together the eggs and the **Carnation** Milk. Season well. Pour the egg mixture over the spinach and cheese. Bake for 30-40 minutes, until golden. Serve warm or cold.

Russian Fish Parcels

Within the shiny, golden pastry hides a delicious mixture of fresh and smoked fish in a creamy sauce.

Serves 6
Preparation time: 20 minutes
Cooking time: 40 minutes

225g (8oz) cod, cubed
225g (8oz) smoked haddock, cubed
1 bay leaf
50g (2oz) butter
1 onion, chopped
50g (2oz) flour
410g can **Carnation** Evaporated Milk
3 eggs, size 2, hard-boiled, chopped
4 tablespoons freshly chopped parsley
450g (1lb) puff pastry
1 egg, beaten
salt and black pepper

1 Preheat the oven to 220°C (425°F), Gas Mark 7.

2 Place the fish and bay leaf in a saucepan and add just enough water to cover. Cover the pan and simmer for 10 minutes or until the fish is cooked. Drain, reserving the cooking liquid and discarding the bay leaf. Cool and flake the fish.

3 Melt the butter in a saucepan, add the onion and cook for 5-10 minutes until softened. Stir in the flour. Add the **Carnation** Milk, and 4 tablespoons of the reserved cooking liquid. Bring to the boil, stirring continuously until thickened. Stir in the chopped eggs, parsley, fish and seasoning.

4 Roll out the pastry until it is 5mm (¼ inch) thick. Cut into six 15cm (6 inch) squares. Divide the filling between the pastry squares. Brush the edges with beaten egg. Fold the pastry edges into the centre and pinch together to form a parcel. Place on a baking sheet and brush with the remaining beaten egg.

5 Bake for 15-20 minutes, then reduce the oven temperature to 180°C (350°F), Gas Mark 4 and cook for a further 10 minutes. Serve hot.

Coconut Chicken Curry

The creamy coconut sauce seems to tone down the spiciness, giving quite a mild curry, but you can always make it hotter by adding chilli powder or chopped fresh chillies with the other spices.

Serves 4-6
Preparation time: 20 minutes
Cooking time: 40 minutes

2 tablespoons oil

675g (1½lb) chicken breast, diced

1 onion, chopped

1 clove garlic, crushed

2.5cm (1inch) piece of fresh root ginger, grated

1 tablespoon ground coriander

2 tablespoons medium Madras curry powder

227g can chopped tomatoes

6 tablespoons dry white wine

300ml (½ pint) chicken stock

pinch of salt

75g (3oz) **Nestlé** Coconut Milk Powder

410g can **Carnation** Evaporated Milk

boiled rice, to serve

shavings of fresh coconut, to garnish

1 Heat the oil in a large saucepan and quickly fry the chicken.

2 Add the onion and garlic and stir-fry for 2 minutes, being careful not to let the garlic burn. Add the ginger, coriander, curry powder, tomatoes, wine and stock. Stir well and season.

3 Cover and simmer for 30 minutes, until the meat is tender.

4 In a bowl mix the **Nestlé** Coconut Milk Powder with the **Carnation** Milk. Add to the pan, stir well, and simmer for 5 minutes. Garnish with the coconut shavings and serve with boiled rice.

NOTE: If you would prefer a spicier curry, try the recipe for Balti Chicken Curry on page 20.

Gratin Dauphinois

Layers of potatoes and onions in a rich, creamy sauce make the perfect accompaniment to plain roast or grilled meat. With its cheese topping, this gratin is also a satisfying lunch or supper dish. Served with green vegetables or a crisp salad.

Serves 4-6
Preparation time: 10 minutes
Cooking time: 1¼ hours

50g (2oz) butter

1 large onion, sliced

675g (1½lb) potatoes, thinly sliced

1 tablespoon flour

410g can **Carnation** Evaporated Milk

100g (4oz) mature Cheddar cheese, grated

salt and freshly ground black pepper

1 Preheat the oven to 200°C (400°F), Gas Mark 6.

2 Melt half the butter in a large frying pan and sauté the onion and potato slices for 5-10 minutes, until golden and lightly softened. Transfer to a shallow gratin dish.

3 Place the remaining butter, flour, **Carnation** Milk, salt and pepper in a small pan over a low heat, whisking continuously until the sauce boils and thickens.

4 Pour the sauce over the potatoes and top with the grated cheese. Cover the dish with foil and bake for 50-60 minutes, until the potatoes are tender. Remove the foil and place the dish under a hot grill until the cheese is bubbling and golden.

Cheese and Onion Tart

This savoury tart is equally good served hot or cold. To take it on a picnic, make it a day ahead and leave in the refrigerator overnight, so that the filling is well set and easy to slice.

Serves 8
Preparation time: 10 minutes
Cooking time: 50-55 minutes

350g (12oz) shortcrust pastry

50g (2oz) butter

2 onions, sliced into rings

225g (8oz) Gruyère or Cheddar cheese, grated

3 eggs, size 2

410g can **Carnation** Evaporated Milk

pinch of ground nutmeg

black pepper

1 Preheat the oven to 200°C (400°F), Gas Mark 6.

2 Roll out the pastry and line a 23cm (9 inch) round, deep, loose-bottomed, fluted flan tin. Chill for 20 minutes, then bake blind (see page 78) for 15 minutes.

3 Melt the butter in a saucepan, add the onions and fry gently for 10 minutes until caramelized. Remove from the heat.

4 Place the cheese, eggs, **Carnation** Milk, nutmeg and pepper in a bowl and whisk lightly until smooth. Stir in the cooked onions and grated cheese. Pour the filling into the pastry case and bake for 30-35 minutes, until the filling sets. Serve warm or cold.

Indulgent Desserts

Coconut Ice Cream

Transport yourself to a tropical island with this superb ice cream. Use it within 2 months.

Serves 4
Preparation time: 10 minutes, plus freezing time
Cooking time: 4-5 minutes

100g (4oz) **Nestlé** Coconut Milk Powder

397g can **Nestlé** Sweetened Condensed Milk

150ml (¼ pint) milk

300ml (½ pint) double cream

1 Place the **Nestlé** Coconut Milk Powder, **Nestlé** Milk and milk in a saucepan and cook over a low heat, stirring occasionally, until the coconut milk powder has completely dissolved. Pour into a freezerproof container and leave to cool.

2 Whip the double cream until stiff, and fold into the coconut mixture. Freeze for 2 hours or until the mixture starts to freeze around the edges.

3 Remove from the freezer and beat with a fork to break up any ice crystals. Return to the freezer until solid. Serve with toasted coconut shavings and lime wedges, or as an accompaniment to fresh fruit such as pineapple.

Bakewell Tart

A traditional English almond tart that can be served cold or warm, with custard or cream.

Serves 8
Preparation time: 20 minutes
Cooking time: 50 minutes

275g (10oz) shortcrust pastry

75g (3oz) butter, at room temperature

75g (3oz) caster sugar

2 eggs, beaten

170g can **Carnation** Evaporated Milk

100g (4oz) ground almonds

½ teaspoon almond essence

25g (1oz) self-raising flour, sifted

5 tablespoons strawberry or raspberry jam

1 Preheat the oven to 190°C (375°F), Gas Mark 5.

2 Roll out the pastry and use to line a 23cm (9 inch) round flan tin. Reserve the trimmings. Bake the pastry case blind (see page 78) for 15 minutes.

3 Beat together the butter and sugar. Beat in the eggs, **Carnation** Milk, almonds and almond essence. Fold in the flour.

4 Spread the jam over the cooked pastry case. Spoon over the creamed mixture. Roll out the reserved pastry and use to make a lattice.

5 Return the tart to the oven and bake for 35 minutes, or until golden.

Chocolate Cups

Delicate chocolate cups filled with a swirl of creamy chocolate filling make a delightful end to a meal, served with coffee.

Makes 6
Preparation time: 15 minutes
Chilling time: 30 minutes

175g (6oz) good-quality plain chocolate

50g (2oz) butter, softened

218g or ½ large (397g) can **Nestlé** Sweetened Condensed Milk

1 tablespoon Greek yogurt

6 chocolate cups (see page 95)

chopped pistachio nuts, to decorate

1 Break the chocolate pieces and place in a small bowl. Allow the chocolate to melt over a pan of simmering water, stirring until smooth (see page 95). Leave to cool slightly.

2 Beat together the butter and **Nestlé** Milk and Greek yogurt, then beat in the melted chocolate and chill for 30 minutes, until the mixture is thick.

3 Spoon the mixture into the cups and decorate with chopped pistachios.

NOTE: Chocolate cups are available in some delicatessens and supermarkets. If you cannot find them, try making your own (see page 95) or alternatively simply serve the chocolate filling in small coffee cups.

The Ultimate Sticky Toffee Pudding

When it comes to rich, sweet puddings, this really is the ultimate! Serve it with its own hot toffee sauce and cool cream or ice cream.

Serves 8
Preparation time: 25 minutes
Cooking time: 45 minutes

50g (2oz) butter, at room temperature

150g (6oz) caster sugar

2 eggs

150g (6oz) stoned dates, chopped

170g can **Carnation** Evaporated Milk

150ml (¼ pint) water

1 teaspoon bicarbonate of soda

150g (6oz) self-raising flour, sifted

175g (7oz) soft brown sugar

TO SERVE

1 quantity toffee sauce (see page 60)

whipped double cream

1 Preheat the oven to 180°C (350°F), Gas Mark 4. Butter a 1.4 litre (2½ pint) shallow ovenproof dish.

2 Beat together the butter and caster sugar. Gradually beat in the eggs.

3 Place the dates, half the can of **Carnation** Milk and the measured water in a saucepan and bring to the boil. Remove from the heat and stir in the bicarbonate of soda.

4 Fold the flour into the egg mixture then stir in the date mixture. Pour the batter into the prepared dish and bake for 35-45 minutes or until a skewer inserted into the centre comes out clean.

5 Serve the pudding warm accompanied by hot toffee sauce (see page 60) and whipped double cream.

Iced Cappuccino Syllabubs

Sweet yet sophisticated, this chilled coffee dessert could also be served in coffee cups.

Serves 6
Preparation time: 30 minutes
Freeze time: 30 minutes

3 tablespoons good quality instant coffee granules, e.g. ***Nescafé** Gold Blend*

3 tablespoons coffee liqueur

397g can **Nestlé** Sweetened Condensed Milk

600ml (1 pint) whipping cream

2 teaspoons caster sugar

a dusting of drinking chocolate, to decorate

1 Dissolve the coffee granules in 3 tablespoons of boiling water and leave to cool. Mix with the coffee liqueur, then whisk into the **Nestlé** Milk.

2 Whip 450ml (¾ pint) of the cream until soft peaks form, then fold into the coffee mixture. Divide the mixture between 6 tall glasses and chill.

3 Meanwhile, place the remaining cream in a bowl with the sugar and 4 tablespoons of ice cold water, and whisk until thick and frothy. Spoon on to the syllabubs and freeze for 30 minutes.

4 To decorate, carefully dust each syllabub with drinking chocolate and serve immediately.

Creamy Almond Rice Pudding

A sumptuous variation on traditional rice pudding, this recipe is also much quicker to make.

Serves 6
Preparation time: 10 minutes
Cooking time: 30 minutes

150g (6oz) pudding rice

finely-grated rind and juice of 1 lemon

100g (4oz) sultanas

1.1 litre (2 pints) water

397g can **Nestlé** Sweetened Condensed Milk

pinch of freshly grated nutmeg

25g (1oz) flaked almonds

icing sugar, to dust

1 Wash the rice thoroughly, drain well and place in a large saucepan with the lemon rind and juice, sultanas and the measured water. Bring to the boil and simmer, uncovered, for 25 minutes.

2 Stir in the **Nestlé** Milk and cook gently over a low heat for 3-4 minutes, stirring occasionally until warmed through.

3 Pour the rice pudding into a warmed serving dish and sprinkle over the freshly grated nutmeg and flaked almonds.

4 Place under a hot grill until the almonds are toasted but be careful not to let them burn. Just before serving, dust with icing sugar.

Rich Chocolate Truffle Torte

Thick chocolate mousse on a biscuit base covered with chocolate curls – absolute bliss for chocolate lovers.

Serves 8-10
Preparation time: 20 minutes
Chilling time: 12 hours or overnight

75g (3oz) butter

150g (6oz) digestive biscuits, crushed

397g can **Nestlé** Sweetened Condensed Milk

450g (1lb) plain chocolate

6 tablespoons brandy

300ml (½ pint) double cream

150g (6oz) plain or milk chocolate curls, to decorate

1 Melt the butter and stir in the crushed biscuits. Press into the base of a 20cm (8 inch) loose-bottomed cake tin and chill.

2 Meanwhile, put the **Nestlé** Milk, chocolate and brandy in a large bowl. Place the bowl over a pan of simmering water and stir until the chocolate has melted (see page 95). Using a hand whisk, beat until smooth. Leave to cool for 5 minutes.

3 Whisk the cream into the chocolate mixture and pour over the biscuit base. Chill for 12 hours or overnight.

4 To make the chocolate curls, melt the plain or milk chocolate (see page 95) and spread on a marble slab or cold metal baking sheet. Chill until just set, then, using a knife or a potato peeler, scrape across the chocolate to make curls.

5 Scatter the chocolate curls over the cake and serve.

Old Fashioned Vanilla Ice Cream

This quick and easy recipe makes a superb ice cream. Create your own variations, such as Ginger Crunch and Strawberries 'n' Cream, or simply serve with a hot or cold sauce (see page 60).

Serves 6
Preparation time: 30 minutes
Freezing time: 2-3 hours

2 × 397g cans **Nestlé** Sweetened Condensed Milk

300ml (½ pint) single cream

200ml (7 fl oz) crème fraîche

1 tablespoon vanilla essence

1 Beat together all the ingredients until smooth and creamy.

2 Transfer to a freezerproof container and freeze until slushy. Beat well then freeze until firm.

3 To serve, leave the ice cream at room temperature to thaw slightly then serve in scoops.

VARIATIONS

Ginger Crunch
At stage *2*, when the ice cream is slushy stir in 150g (6oz) roughly crushed ginger biscuits. Then continue as above.

Strawberries 'n' Cream
At stage *2* when the ice cream is slushy, lightly stir in 150g (6oz) puréed fresh or canned strawberries, to create a rippled effect. Then continue as above.

Crème Caramel

Silky-smooth crème caramels are a delightful and ever-popular way to end a meal.

Makes 6
Preparation time: 10 minutes
Cooking time: 50 minutes
Chilling time: 1 hour

100g (4oz) caster sugar

397g can **Nestlé** Sweetened Condensed Milk

4 eggs, beaten

1 tablespoon vanilla essence

1 Preheat the oven to 180°C (350°F), Gas Mark 4.

2 Place the caster sugar in a heavy-bottomed saucepan, over a medium heat. Do not stir. Watch the sugar until the bottom layer turns to liquid. Reduce the heat and stir until all the sugar has dissolved and turned a light caramel colour. Remove from the heat and continue stirring for 1-2 minutes. (This allows the caramel to cool and prevents the caramel turning too dark). Pour into 6 ramekin dishes, about 7.5cm (3 inches) in diameter.

3 Whisk the remaining ingredients together with 300ml (½ pint) water. Strain into the ramekins.

4 Stand the ramekins in a roasting pan, then pour boiling water into the roasting pan, to come two-thirds of the way up the sides of the ramekins. Cover the roasting pan loosely with foil and bake for 40 minutes, then remove the foil and bake for a further 10 minutes, or until set.

5 Leave the crème caramels to cool, then chill for about 1 hour. To serve, turn out on to individual plates.

NOTE: You don't need special ramekin dishes; teacups are fine, but don't use bone china, because the hot caramel might crack them.

Spun Sugar Decoration
Using an additional 100g (4oz) of caster sugar, follow the method for stage *2*. When the syrup is a light caramel colour, instead of pouring it into the ramekin dishes, remove from the heat and using a spoon immediately drizzle 6 thin 'squiggly-shaped' decorations on to a piece of greaseproof paper. Leave in a cool place to set. Just before serving carefully remove the spun sugar decorations from the greaseproof paper and place one on top of each crème caramel.

Caramelized Bread and Butter Pudding

A traditional English pudding is given a new look with a caramelized sugar topping.

Serves 4-6
Preparation time: 30 minutes
Cooking time: 30 minutes

150g (6oz) brioche, cut into thin slices and buttered

50g (2oz) sultanas

3 egg yolks

75g (3oz) caster sugar

410g can **Carnation** Evaporated Milk

2 tablespoons caster sugar, to finish

1 Preheat the oven to 180°C (350°F), Gas Mark 4.

2 Arrange the buttered brioche in layers in a 1 litre (1¾ pint) ovenproof dish, sprinkling each layer with sultanas.

3 Whisk together the egg yolks and sugar, then stir in the **Carnation** Milk. Pour over the brioche and leave to soak for 20 minutes.

4 Place the dish in a roasting pan, then pour boiling water into the roasting pan, to come two-thirds of the way up the side of the dish. Bake for 30 minutes or until set.

5 Sprinkle with caster sugar and place under a hot grill until the sugar caramelizes.

Banoffi Pie

It takes only 10 minutes for the milk to caramelize in this delicious caramel and banana pie, which is always popular with the sweet-toothed.

Serves 8
Preparation time: 20 minutes
Chilling time: 1½ hours

275g (10oz) butter

250g (9oz) gingernut biscuits, crushed

150g (6oz) caster sugar

397g can **Nestlé** Sweetened Condensed Milk

2 bananas

150ml (¼ pint) double cream, whipped

plain chocolate, grated, to decorate

1 In a large saucepan, melt 100g (4oz) of the butter and stir in the crushed biscuits. Press into the base and sides of a 19cm (7½ inch) deep, loose-bottomed fluted, flan tin. Chill for 30 minutes.

2 Place the remaining butter and the sugar in a nonstick saucepan over a low heat, stirring until the butter melts. Add the **Nestlé** Milk and bring gently to the boil, stirring continuously. Boil steadily for exactly 5 minutes, stirring frequently, to make a light golden caramel.

3 Pour over the biscuit base and chill for about 1 hour, until firm.

4 To serve, slice the bananas and arrange most of them over the caramel. Spread with the whipped cream. Decorate with the remaining bananas and grated chocolate.

Tiramisu

This dessert derives its name from the Italian for 'pick-me-up', because of the brandy and strong coffee used as flavourings.

Serves 6-8
Preparation time: 30 minutes
Chilling time: 30 minutes

397g can **Nestlé** Sweetened Condensed Milk

450g (1lb) mascarpone cheese

3 tablespoons Marsala wine or brandy

150ml (¼ pint) cold strong black coffee

100g (4oz) sponge fingers

2 tablespoons cocoa powder

1 In a mixing bowl, beat together the **Nestlé** Milk and mascarpone.

2 In a shallow dish, mix together the Marsala wine or brandy with the coffee. Take one sponge finger at a time, and dip it into the coffee mixture, holding it in for a few seconds but taking care not to let it become soggy.

3 Line a trifle dish with half the coffee-dipped sponge fingers. Spoon over half the milk and cheese mixture. Sift over a generous dusting of cocoa.

4 Cover with another layer of sponge fingers, cream and cocoa, then chill for at least 30 minutes before serving.

NOTE: Mascarpone is a rich smooth Italian cream cheese available in supermarkets and delicatessens.

Make puddings extra-special; with these easy-to-make chocolate and toffee sauces, or creamy-tasting custard.

Carnation Toffee Sauce

Makes about 300ml (½ pint)
Preparation time: 2 minutes
Cooking time: 5 minutes

50g (2oz) butter

175g (7oz) soft brown sugar

170g can **Carnation** Evaporated Milk

1 Place all the ingredients in a nonstick saucepan over a low heat until the butter has melted.

2 Bring gently to the boil, stirring continuously. Boil for 2-5 minutes, until the sauce thickens.

3 Serve immediately with a hot sponge pudding (Sticky Toffee Pudding, see recipe on page 42) or ice cream (Old Fashioned Vanilla Ice Cream, see recipe on page 50).

Carnation Custard

Makes approximately 600ml (1 pint)
Preparation time: 2 minutes
Cooking time: 5 minutes

410g can **Carnation** Evaporated Milk

1 vanilla pod
or 2 teaspoons vanilla essence

2 tablespoons caster sugar

2 tablespoons custard powder

1 Place the **Carnation** Milk, vanilla pod or essence and sugar in a saucepan.

2 Blend the custard powder with water to form a paste.

3 Add the custard paste to the pan and place over a low heat, whisking continuously until the custard has boiled and thickened. Remove the vanilla pod, if using and serve immediately.

Carnation Chocolate Sauce

Makes about 300ml (½ pint)
Preparation time: 2 minutes
Cooking time: 5 minutes

150g (6oz) plain chocolate

170g can **Carnation** Evaporated Milk

1 Break the chocolate into pieces and place in a bowl with the **Carnation** Milk.

2 Stand the bowl over a saucepan of simmering water and stir until the chocolate has melted and the mixture is smooth.

3 Serve warm over puddings or ice cream. Alternatively leave to cool and thicken slightly and use as a cake covering (Gooey Chocolate Brownies, see page 88).

Coconut Jelly with Oriental Fruits

A selection of bright juicy, exotic fruit is made into a special dessert when served with a cool coconut jelly.

Serves 6
Preparation time: 20 minutes
Chilling time: up to 3 hours

170g can **Carnation** Evaporated Milk

5 tablespoons **Nestlé** Coconut Milk Powder

300ml (½ pint) water

2 tablespoons gelatine

175g (7oz) caster sugar

4 egg whites

TO SERVE

a selection of exotic fruit, e.g. star fruit, mangosteen, kiwifruit, lychees, Cape gooseberries (physalis), pomegranates.

1 Mix together the **Carnation** Milk and **Nestlé** Coconut Milk Powder.

2 Place the water, gelatine and sugar in a pan and heat, stirring until the gelatine and sugar have dissolved.

3 Stir in the **Carnation** Milk mixture and leave to cool for 1-2 hours, stirring occasionally.

4 Whisk the egg whites until stiff and fold into the coconut mixture. Rinse an 18cm (7 inch) square cake tin in cold water, spoon in the coconut mixture and chill until set.

5 Prepare the selection of fruit as necessary and place it around the coconut jelly. Cut the jelly into squares when serving.

Bruléed Mandarin and Banana Trifle

Everyone loves a homemade trifle and its a great pudding to make ahead of time. Don't grill the sugar topping too far in advance, however or the caramel will soften.

Serves 4-6
Preparation time: 30 minutes
Chilling time: 1¼ hours

2 x 298g cans mandarins in natural juice, drained, reserving the juice from 1 can

3 tablespoons brandy

2 bananas, sliced

125g (5oz) Madeira cake, sliced thinly

150ml (¼ pint) double cream, whipped

600ml (1 pint) **Carnation** Custard, chilled, (see page 60)

50g (2oz) soft brown sugar, to finish

1 Place the mandarins in a bowl with the reserved juice and brandy. Leave to stand for 30 minutes.

2 Layer the mandarins, bananas and Madeira cake in a heatproof, 1.1 litre (2 pint) serving bowl, soaking the cake in the juices.

3 Beat the cold custard briefly then fold in the whipped cream. Spoon over the trifle. Sprinkle the surface with the brown sugar, then chill for at least 45 minutes.

4 To finish, place under a hot grill until the sugar caramelizes. Chill for a further 30 minutes before serving.

Apricot Flan

A fruit tart that looks – and tastes – as good as those in any French pastry shop. Fresh apricots provide a good contrast to the creamy filling; you could substitute unsweetened canned apricots in natural juice – but be sure to drain them well and pat dry with paper towels.

Serves 6-8
Preparation time: 40 minutes
Chilling time: 20-30 minutes
Cooking time: 1 hour

175g (7oz) plain flour

125g (5oz) butter, at room temperature

1 tablespoon icing sugar

FILLING

2 whole eggs, plus 1 egg yolk

170g can **Carnation** Evaporated Milk

50g (2oz) icing sugar

½ teaspoon grated nutmeg

25g (1oz) white breadcrumbs

8-10 fresh, ripe apricots, halved and stoned

5 tablespoons apricot jam, warmed and sieved, to glaze

1 Preheat the oven to 200°C (400°F), Gas Mark 6.

2 Place the flour, butter and 1 tablespoon of icing sugar in a food processor and process until crumbs form; alternatively rub the ingredients together by hand. Press into the base and sides of a 20.5 x 28cm (8 x 11 inch) loose-bottomed flan tin. Chill for 20-30 minutes. Bake blind for 10-15 minutes (see page 78). Leave to cool. Reduce the oven temperature to 180°C (350°F), Gas Mark 4.

3 Whisk together the eggs, **Carnation** Milk, icing sugar and nutmeg.

4 Scatter the breadcrumbs over the base of the flan case and arrange the apricots on top. Pour over the milk mixture. Bake the tart for 50 minutes or until the apricots have softened. Brush with the jam and serve warm.

Key Lime Pie

Originally from Florida, where limes grow wild on the small islands known as keys. Limes are stronger than lemons and give a refreshing tang to this pie.

Serves 6-8
Preparation time: 20 minutes
Chilling time: 1 hour

75g (3oz) butter

225g (8oz) digestive biscuits, crushed

300ml (½ pint) double cream

juice and rind of 4 large limes

218g can **Nestlé** Sweetened Condensed Milk

TO DECORATE

whipped cream and lime slices

1 Melt the butter, stir in the crushed biscuits. Press into the base and sides of a 20.5cm (8 inch) deep, loose-bottomed, fluted flan tin. Chill.

2 For the filling, whisk together the remaining ingredients until thick and creamy. Spoon over the biscuit base.

3 Chill, then just before serving, pipe the whipped cream around the edge of the pie and decorate with the lime slices.

Whisked Lemon Milk Jelly

A childhood favourite milk jelly, becomes a grown-up dessert served in elegant glasses. It would also look impressive made in an old-fashioned jelly mould and turned out.

Serves 4
Preparation time: 10 minutes
Chilling time: 45 minutes

1 packet of lemon jelly

150ml (¼ pint) boiling water

grated rind and juice of 1 large lemon

410g can **Carnation** Evaporated Milk, chilled

TO DECORATE

orange or lemon slices and grated orange or lemon rind

1 Dissolve the jelly in the boiling water and stir in the lemon rind and juice. Leave to cool slightly.

2 Meanwhile, whisk the **Carnation** Milk ideally with an electric hand whisk until doubled in volume, then gradually whisk in the cooled jelly.

3 Transfer to a jug and pour into 4 tall glasses. Chill until set.

4 To serve, decorate with the orange and lemon rind.

NOTE: For a special occasion whisk in a 200g (7oz) carton of crème fraîche when adding the cooled jelly.

VARIATIONS: This recipe can be adapted to use a variety of flavours. Simply substitute the packet of lemon jelly with your favourite fruit jelly, omit the lemon rind and decorate with your chosen fruit.

Apple Delight

This apple batter pudding is perfect served warm as a dessert, or cold and cut into pieces for teatime.

Serves 6
Preparation time: 15 minutes
Cooking time: 20-25 minutes

2-3 cooking apples
2 eggs, beaten
250g (9oz) caster sugar
100g (4oz) butter
410g can **Carnation** Evaporated Milk
175g (7oz) plain flour, sifted
2 teaspoons baking powder

1 Preheat the oven to 200°C (400°F), Gas Mark 6. Grease a nonstick roasting pan, measuring 25.5 x 30.5cm (10 x 12 inches).

2 Peel, core and slice the apples and cover with water to prevent them from browning.

3 Whisk the eggs and 225g (8oz) of caster sugar until thick and creamy. Place the butter and half the can of **Carnation** Milk in a small saucepan and heat until the butter has melted. Stir this into the egg mixture.

4 Fold in the flour and baking powder. Pour into the prepared tin.

5 Drain the apple slices, pat dry and arrange on top of the batter. Sprinkle on the remaining sugar.

6 Bake for 20-25 minutes until golden. Cut into slices and serve with the remaining **Carnation** Milk.

Carnation Yogurt

Serve this mild, creamy-tasting yogurt with fresh fruits for a delicious dessert or breakfast.

Serves 4
Preparation time: 5 minutes
Setting time: 3 hours

410g can **Carnation** Evaporated Milk

2 tablespoons dried skimmed milk powder

2 tablespoons live natural yogurt

TO DECORATE

summer fruits, such as raspberries, blackberries and strawberries

1 Pour the **Carnation** Milk into a 1.1 litre (2 pint) measuring jug and make up to 900ml (1½ pint) with warm boiled water.

2 Whisk in the dried milk and the yogurt and pour into an electric yogurt maker or large warmed thermos flask. Either method will take about 3 hours for the yogurt to set.

3 Should the yogurt not be quite as thick as required, add a little extra dried milk powder. The yogurt will thicken slightly on storage. Store in the refrigerator.

4 Decorate with the summer fruits just before serving.

Raspberry-Ripple Cheesecake

When they are in season, use fresh raspberries to make this stunning cheesecake.

Serves 8
Preparation time: 20 minutes
Chilling time: 1½-2½ hours

75g (3oz) butter

150g (6oz) digestive biscuits, crushed

6 tablespoons lemon juice

5 teaspoons gelatine

225g (8oz) fresh or frozen raspberries

200g (7oz) cream cheese

300ml (½ pint) soured cream

397g can **Nestlé** Sweetened Condensed Milk

fresh raspberries, to decorate

1 Melt the butter in a saucepan. Stir in the crushed biscuits. Press the mixture into the base of a 20.5cm (8 inch) round, loose-bottomed cake tin. Chill.

2 Meanwhile, place the lemon juice in a small bowl. Sprinkle over the gelatine. Leave to stand for 10 minutes, then place the bowl over a pan of simmering water, stirring occasionally, until the gelatine has dissolved. Leave to cool.

3 Purée half the raspberries, rub through a sieve and reserve.

4 Beat together the cream cheese, soured cream and **Nestlé** Milk, then stir in the cooled gelatine.

5 Carefully fold in the raspberries and purée to create a rippled effect. Spoon over the biscuit base and chill for 1½-2½ hours, until set.

6 Just before serving decorate with fresh raspberries.

Glazed Lemon Tart

Deliciously tangy, with a golden brown, caramelized sugar glaze, this elegant tart is incredibly easy to make.

Serves 6-8
Preparation time: 25 minutes
Cooking time: 40-60 minutes

225g (8oz) sweet pastry crumbs (see Apricot Flan, page 66)

6 egg yolks

275g (10oz) caster sugar

grated rind and juice of 3 lemons

170g can **Carnation** Evaporated Milk

4 tablespoons icing sugar, to finish

1 Preheat the oven to 220°C (425°F), Gas Mark 7.

2 Press the pastry crumbs into a 28cm (11 inch) round, fluted flan tin. Chill for 20-30 minutes then bake blind (see Note opposite) for 15-20 minutes, until crisp.

3 For the filling, mix the egg yolks and caster sugar together until smooth. Stir in the lemon rind and juice and **Carnation** Milk. Pour into the pastry case and bake for 30-40 minutes, until just set.

4 Leave to cool completely and chill until ready to serve.

5 To serve, sprinkle the tart with the icing sugar and place under a hot grill, for 2-3 minutes. Watch continuously and turn as necessary, until the sugar browns, without letting it burn.

NOTE:

Baking Blind
Line the flan tin with a large circle of greaseproof paper. Fill with baking beans or pasta (these can be saved and used again for the same purpose). Alternatively use a piece of crumpled foil. Bake in a preheated oven for the time indicated in the recipe, then remove the paper and the beans.

Lemon Meringue Pie

Next time you make lemon meringue pie, try this simple yet effective recipe.

Serves 6
Preparation time: 15 minutes
Cooking time: 15-20 minutes

50g (2oz) butter

150g (6oz) digestive biscuits, crushed

397g can **Nestlé** Sweetened Condensed Milk

2 eggs, separated

grated rind and juice of 2 lemons

100g (4oz) caster sugar

1 Preheat the oven to 190°C (375°F), Gas Mark 5.

2 Melt the butter and stir in the crushed biscuits. Press the mixture into the base and sides of a 20.5cm (8 inch) round, fluted flan dish.

3 Beat together the **Nestlé** Milk, egg yolks, lemon rind and juice. Pour over the biscuit base.

4 Whisk the egg whites until soft peaks form, then gradually whisk in the caster sugar until the mixture is stiff. Pile the meringue on top of the lemon filling and bake for 15-20 minutes until the meringue is golden and crisp.

Raspberry and Amaretto Fools

An intriguing combination of flavour go into this elegant dessert. If you like, accompany it with whole Amaretto biscuits.

Serves 6
Preparation time: 15 minutes
Chilling time: 45 minutes

350g (12oz) fresh or frozen raspberries

2 tablespoons almond liqueur, e.g. Amaretto di Saronno

218g or ½ large (397g) can **Nestlé** Sweetened Condensed Milk

150ml (¼ pint) natural yogurt

300ml (½ pint) double cream, whipped

100g (4oz) Amaretti or ratafia biscuits, lightly crushed

fresh raspberries, to decorate

1 Place all the ingredients except the double cream and biscuits into a liquidizer or food processor and blend until smooth.

2 Rub the mixture through a sieve to remove the raspberry seeds, then fold in the whipped cream.

3 Divide the crushed biscuits between 6 tall glasses, then spoon over the raspberry fool. Chill.

4 Just before serving decorate with the fresh raspberries.

Gooey Chocolate Brownies

One of the all-time favourite chocolate recipes, these brownies are sticky, fudge-like, and very, very chocolaty.

Makes 12
Preparation time: 30 minutes
Cooking time: 1 hour 20 minutes

225g (8oz) plain chocolate
150g (6oz) butter
150g (6oz) caster sugar
150g (6oz) ground almonds
6 eggs, size 2, separated
150g (6oz) fresh white breadcrumbs
170g can **Carnation** Evaporated Milk
4 tablespoons cocoa powder
125g (5oz) white chocolate, chopped
125g (5oz) milk chocolate, chopped
300ml (½ pint) cooled chocolate sauce (page 60), to serve

1 Preheat the oven to 180°C (350°F), Gas Mark 4. Grease and line a 20.5cm (8 inch) square cake tin.

2 Melt the plain chocolate in a bowl over a pan of simmering water (see page 95).

3 Meanwhile, beat together the butter and sugar until light and fluffy. Stir in the almonds, egg yolks, breadcrumbs, **Carnation** Milk, cocoa and melted plain chocolate.

4 Whisk the egg whites until soft peaks form. Fold into the chocolate mixture, together with the chopped white and milk chocolate.

5 Spoon the mixture into the prepared tin and bake for 1 hour 20 minutes. Turn out and cool on a wire rack.

6 Cut the cake into 12 squares and serve piled on a plate and drizzled with the chocolate sauce.

Homemade sweets seem to taste so much better than shop-bought ones. Here is a selection of classic sweet recipes that make wonderful gifts or treats.

Toffee Crispies

Makes 20
Preparation time: 10 minutes
Cooking time: 10 minutes

75g (3oz) butter

125g (5oz) sugar

397g can **Nestlé** Sweetened Condensed Milk

1 tablespoon golden syrup

50g (2oz) crisp puffed rice

1 Lightly grease an 18cm (7 inch) square tin.

2 Melt the butter and sugar together in a large saucepan. Add the **Nestlé** Milk and golden syrup. Heat gently, stirring continuously and bring to the boil. Simmer for 5 minutes.

3 Stir in the puffed rice and pour into the prepared tin. Leave to set in a cool place.

4 When cool cut the toffee crispies into squares. Store in an airtight container for up to a week.

Black Jack Toffee

Makes 1.35kg (3lb)
Preparation time: 5 minutes
Cooking time: 35-40 minutes

350g (12oz) margarine

225g (8oz) black treacle

[illegible]g (1lb) dark brown sugar

397g can **Nestlé** Sweetened Condensed Milk

1 Grease a 23 x 30.5cm (9 x 12 inch) baking tin.

2 Melt the margarine in a non-stick saucepan. Add the sugar, treacle and **Nestlé** Milk.

3 Bring slowly to the boil and simmer for 35-40 minutes, stirring constantly to a temperature of 132°C (270°F), using a sugar thermometer. Alternatively, follow the test for soft crack on page 95.

4 Pour into the tin. Chill until set, turn out and break into pieces using a toffee hammer or a rolling pin.

Coconut Ice

Makes 1.25kg (2½lb)
Preparation time: 15 minutes

397g can **Nestlé** Sweetened Condensed Milk

500g (1lb 2oz) icing sugar, sifted, plus extra to dust

350g (12oz) desiccated coconut

few drops of red food colouring

1 Mix together the **Nestlé** Milk and the icing sugar. Stir in the coconut (mixture should be stiff) and divide in half.

2 Colour half of the mixture pale pink, using a few drops of red food colouring.

3 Shape the pink and white mixtures into two identically shaped bars and press firmly together. Dust a chopping board with icing sugar and leave the coconut ice on it until firm. Cut into pieces. Store in an airtight container for 2-3 weeks.

Chocolate Truffles

Serve these truffles with coffee to provide a note of luxury, or pack them into pretty boxes to give as presents.

Makes 20-25
Preparation time: 20-30 minutes
Chilling time: 30-45 minutes

150g (6oz) plain chocolate, melted

170g can **Nestlé** Cream

3 tablespoons rum (optional)

175g (7oz) cake crumbs

50g (2oz) ground almonds

chocolate vermicelli, grated chocolate or cocoa powder, to finish

1 Leave the chocolate to cool slightly, then beat in the **Nestlé** Cream and rum, if using, until smooth.

2 Gradually beat in the cake crumbs and ground almonds. Then chill, for 30-45 minutes.

3 Divide the mixture into 20-25 balls. Roll the balls in the chocolate vermicelli, grated chocolate or cocoa powder then place in petit four cases.

NOTE: See page 95 on how to melt chocolate successfully.

Making your own sweets

Nestlé Milk is ideal for making confectionery. Here are some invaluable hints that will help ensure that your toffees and fudges always look and taste absolutely delicious.

◆ Choose a heavy-bottomed saucepan; most old nonstick saucepans are not suitable because the nonstick coating may crack.

◆ Fudge and toffee mixtures rise during boiling, so choose a saucepan which is no more than half full, once all the ingredients have been added.

◆ Always heat the mixture slowly until the sugar has completely dissolved.

◆ Use a plastic heatproof spoon for stirring the toffee or fudge: a metal spoon will conduct heat and the handle will become too hot to hold.

◆ A sugar thermometer is the most accurate way to test the setting point for fudge or toffee. Alternatively the temperature can be estimated by using the tests described on page 95.

◆ Once setting point is reached, leave the fudge mixture to cool for 5 minutes, then beat well with a plastic heatproof spoon, until the mixture is thick and grainy. Do not use an electric whisk to beat fudge. Never beat the mixture when hot or large sugar crystals will form and spoil the fudge. Pour the beaten fudge mixture into a well-oiled tray.

◆ Plunge empty saucepans into hot soapy water to dissolve the sugar mixture for easy cleaning.

◆ Store fudge and toffee in airtight containers.

Sugar syrups

Basic sugar syrups are used in many different ways – for poaching fruit, making fruit salads, ice creams, sorbets and jellies; when sugar is boiled to higher temperatures it can be used to make a range of sweets.

When making sugar syrups or caramels, it is better to use coarse-grained or lump sugar which hold fewer impurities and give a clearer result.

The amount of sugar used can vary from 75–125g (3–4oz) per 300ml (½ pint) water for a light syrup (for poaching fruit) to 500g (1lb) sugar to 150ml (¼ pint) water for heavy syrup (for fondant).

Care must be taken when dissolving the sugar in water to ensure that the sugar does not crystallize in the boiling syrup. Always heat the mixture gently until the sugar dissolves, the liquid is then boiled to form a syrup which is used as required.

When sugar syrups are boiled to high temperatures they will begin to change colour and turn into caramel. Caramel may be allowed to set hard and crushed to add texture (to ice creams, for example), or it can be used for decoration or shaped into baskets. If a small amount of hot water is added to the hot caramel it will prevent it from setting, and will form a caramel syrup.

Sugar boiling chart

A sugar thermometer is the most accurate way to monitor the various stages when boiling sugar syrup. Always ensure the temperature is read from the centre of the mixture and take care that the thermometer does not rest on the saucepan base. If a sugar thermometer is not available the temperature can be estimated by using the following tests.

TEMPERATURE	USES
Thread: 107°C/225°F Using a small spoon or fork, remove a little of the syrup and allow it to fall from the spoon or fork. It should form a fine thin thread.	**Sorbet**
Soft ball: 113–118°C /235–245°F Drop a small amount of the syrup into iced water. Mould the sticky syrup into a soft ball with the fingers. Remove the ball from the water. It should immediately lose its shape.	**Fudge; fondant**
Hard ball: 120–130°C/248–266°F Drop a little syrup into iced water, then mould into a ball and remove from the water. It should feel firm and quite sticky.	**Butterscotch**
Soft crack: 132–142°C/270–286°F Drop a little syrup into iced water. Remove from the water and gently stretch it between the fingers. It should form hard but elastic strands, and feel only slightly sticky.	**Soft toffee; frosting**
Hard crack: 149–154°C/300–310°F Drop a little syrup into iced water. Remove from the water. It should form brittle threads which snap easily between the fingers.	**Hard toffee**
Caramel: 160–177°C/320–350°F Using a small spoon pour a little syrup on to a white saucer. It should be a light golden brown.	**Sauces; crème caramel**

Chocolate

Melting chocolate

To melt chocolate successfully, put pieces of chocolate in the top of a double boiler, or in a heatproof bowl that will fit securely over a saucepan. Partially fill the pan with water – the water must not touch the bottom of the bowl. Bring the water almost to the boil, remove from the heat, and place the bowl containing the chocolate over the pan. With a spoon, break up the chocolate as it melts, then stir until smooth.

Chocolate can be melted in a microwave. Put the chocolate pieces in a glass bowl, place in the microwave and cook for 1 minute at full power. Stir, then cook for a further minute until the chocolate is shiny on top.

Chocolate Cups

Melt 350g (12oz) of good-quality plain chocolate (see above). Cover the outsides of 6 tea cups with foil. Dip each cup into the melted chocolate and leave in a cool place until set. Each cup will need to be dipped 2-3 times. Once set carefully remove the foil. (See recipe on page 40).

Index